Cuthbert

higher-level thinking
Questions

Personal & Social Skills

questions by
Miguel Kagan

created and designed by
Miguel Kagan

illustrated by
Celso Rodriguez

Kagan

Kagan Publishing
P.O. Box 72008
San Clemente, CA 92673-2008
1(800) 933-2667
www.KaganOnline.com

ISBN: 978-1-879097-55-1

Table of Contents

I had six
honest serving men
They taught me all I knew:
Their names were Where
and What and When
and Why and How and
Who.

— Rudyard Kipling

Higher-Level Thinking Questions for Personal and Social Skills
Kagan Publishing • 1 (800) 933-2667 • www.KaganOnline.com

Introduction

In your hands you hold a powerful book. It is a member of a series of transformative blackline activity books. Between the covers, you will find questions, questions, and more questions! But these are no ordinary questions. These are the important kind—higher-level thinking questions—the kind that stretch your students' minds; the kind that release your students' natural curiosity about the world; the kind that rack your students' brains; the kind that instill in your students a sense of wonderment about your curriculum.

But we are getting a bit ahead of ourselves. Let's start from the beginning. Since this is a book of questions, it seems only appropriate for this introduction to pose a few questions—about the book and its underlying educational philosophy. So Mr. Kipling's Six Honest Serving Men, if you will, please lead the way:

What?
What are higher-level thinking questions?

This is a loaded question (as should be all good questions). Using our analytic thinking skills, let's break this question down into two smaller questions: 1) What is higher-level thinking? and 2) What are questions? When we understand the types of thinking skills and the types of questions, we can combine the best of both worlds, crafting beautiful questions to generate the range of higher-level thinking in our students!

Types of Thinking
There are many different types of thinking. Some types of thinking include:

- applying
- associating
- comparing
- contrasting
- defining
- elaborating
- empathizing
- experimenting
- generalizing
- investigating
- making analogies
- planning
- prioritizing
- recalling
- reflecting
- reversing
- sequencing
- summarizing
- synthesizing
- assessing
- augmenting
- connecting
- decision-making
- drawing conclusions
- eliminating
- evaluating
- explaining
- inferring consequences
- inventing
- memorizing
- predicting
- problem-solving
- reducing
- relating
- role-taking
- substituting
- symbolizing
- understanding
- thinking about thinking (metacognition)

This is quite a formidable list. It's nowhere near complete. Thinking is a big, multifaceted phenomenon. Perhaps the most widely recognized system for classifying thinking and classroom questions is Benjamin Bloom's Taxonomy of Thinking Skills. Bloom's Taxonomy classifies thinking skills into six hierarchical levels. It begins with the lower levels of thinking skills and moves up to higher-level thinking skills: 1) Knowledge, 2) Comprehension, 3) Application, 4) Analysis, 5) Synthesis, 6) Evaluation. See Bloom's Taxonomy on the following page.

Higher-Level Thinking Questions for Personal and Social Skills
Kagan Publishing • 1 (800) 933-2667 • www.KaganOnline.com

3

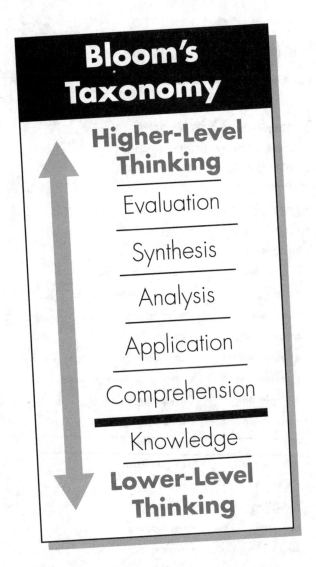

Bloom's Taxonomy

Higher-Level Thinking

Evaluation

Synthesis

Analysis

Application

Comprehension

Knowledge

Lower-Level Thinking

In education, the term "higher-level thinking" often refers to the higher levels of Mr. Bloom's taxonomy. But Bloom's Taxonomy is but one way of organizing and conceptualizing the various types of thinking skills.

There are many ways we can cut the thinking skills pie. We can alternatively view the many different types of thinking skills as, well…many different skills. Some thinking skills may be hierarchical. Some may be interrelated. And some may be relatively independent.

In this book, we take a pragmatic, functional approach. Each type of thinking skill serves a different function. So called "lower-level" thinking skills are very useful for certain purposes. Memorizing and understanding information

are invaluable skills that our students will use throughout their lives. But so too are many of the "higher-level" thinking skills on our list. The more facets of students' thinking skills we develop, the better we prepare them for lifelong success.

Because so much classroom learning heretofore has focused on the "lower rungs" of the thinking skills ladder—knowledge and comprehension, or memorization and understanding—in this series of books we have chosen to focus on questions to generate "higher-level" thinking. This book is an attempt to correct the imbalance in the types of thinking skills developed by classroom questions.

Types of Questions
As we ask questions of our students, we further promote cognitive development when we use Fat questions, Low-Consensus questions, and True questions.

Fat Questions vs. Skinny Questions
Skinny questions are questions that require a skinny answer. For example, after reading a poem, we can ask: "Did you like the poem?" Even though this question could be categorized as an Evaluation question—Bloom's highest level of thinking—it can be answered with one monosyllabic word: "Yes" or "No." How much thinking are we actually generating in our students?

We can reframe this question to make it a fat question: "What things did you like about the poem? What things did you dislike?" Notice no short answer will do. Answering this fattened-up question requires more elaboration. These fat questions presuppose not that there is only one thing but things plural that the student liked and things that she did not like. Making things plural is one way to make skinny questions fat. Students stretch their minds to come up with multiple ideas or solutions. Other easy ways to make questions fat is to add "Why or why not?" or "Explain" or "Describe" or "Defend your position" to the end of a question. These additions promote elaboration beyond a skinny answer. Because language and thought are intimately intertwined, questions that require elaborate responses stretch students' thinking: They grapple to articulate their thoughts.

The type of questions we ask impact not just the type of thinking we develop in our students, but also the depth of thought. Fat questions elicit fat responses. Fat responses develop both depth of thinking and range of thinking skills. The questions in this book are designed to elicit fat responses—deep and varied thinking.

High-Consensus Questions vs. Low-Consensus Questions

A high-consensus question is one to which most people would give the same response, usually a right or wrong answer. After learning about sound, we can ask our students: "What is the name of a room specially designed to improve acoustics for the audience?" This is a high-consensus question. The answer (auditorium) is either correct or incorrect.

Compare the previous question with a low-consensus question: "If you were going to build an auditorium, what special design features would you take into consideration?" Notice, to the low-consensus question there is no right or wrong answer. Each person formulates his or her unique response. To answer, students must apply what they learned, use their ingenuity and creativity.

High-consensus questions promote convergent thinking. With high-consensus questions we strive to direct students **what to think**. Low-consensus questions promote divergent thinking, both critical and creative. With low-consensus

questions we strive to develop students' **ability to think**. The questions in this book are low-consensus questions designed to promote independent, critical and creative thought.

True Questions vs. Review Questions

We all know what review questions are. They're the ones in the back of every chapter and unit. Review questions ask students to regurgitate previously stated or learned information. For example, after learning about the rain forest we may ask: "What percent of the world's oxygen does the rain forest produce?" Students can go back a few pages in their books or into their memory banks and pull out the answer. This is great if we are working on memorization skills, but does little to develop "higher-order" thinking skills.

True questions, on the other hand, are meaningful questions—questions to which we do not know the answer. For example: "What might happen if all the world's rain forests were cut down?" This is a hypothetical; we don't know the answer but considering the question forces us to think. We infer some logical consequences based on what we know. The goal of true questions is not a correct answer, but the thinking journey students take to create a meaningful response. True questions are more representative of real life. Seldom is there a black and white answer. In life, we struggle with ambiguity, confounding variables, and uncertain outcomes. There are millions of shades of gray. True questions prepare students to deal with life's uncertainties.

When we ask a review question, we know the answer and are checking to see if the student does also. When we ask a true question, it is truly a question. We don't necessarily know the answer and neither does the student. True questions are

> # Education is not the filling of a pail, but the lighting of a fire.
> — William Butler Yeats

Higher-Level Thinking Questions for Personal and Social Skills
Kagan Publishing • 1 (800) 933-2667 • www.KaganOnline.com

5

Types of Questions

Skinny ➡️	**Fat**
• Short Answer	• Elaborated Answer
• Shallow Thinking	• Deep Thinking
High-Consensus ➡️	**Low-Consensus**
• Right or Wrong Answer	• No Single Correct Answer
• Develops Convergent Thinking	• Develops Divergent Thinking
• "What" to Think	• "How" to Think
Review ➡️	**True**
• Asker Knows Answer	• Asker Doesn't Know Answer
• Checking for Correctness	• Invitation to Think

often an invitation to think, ponder, speculate, and engage in a questioning process.

We can use true questions in the classroom to make our curriculum more personally meaningful, to promote investigation, and awaken students' sense of awe and wonderment in what we teach. Many questions you will find in this book are true questions designed to make the content provocative, intriguing, and personally relevant.

The box above summarizes the different types of questions. The questions you will find in this book are a move away from skinny, high-consensus, review questions toward fat, low-consensus true questions. As we ask these types of questions in our class, we transform even mundane content into a springboard for higher-level thinking. As we integrate these question gems into our daily lessons, we create powerful learning experiences. ***We do not fill our students' pails with knowledge; we kindle their fires to become lifetime thinkers.***

Why?
Why should I use higher-level thinking questions in my classroom?

As we enter the new millennium, major shifts in our economic structure are changing the ways we work and live. The direction is increasingly toward an information-based, high-tech economy. The sum of our technological information is exploding. We could give you a figure how rapidly information is doubling, but by the time you read this, the number would be outdated! No kidding.

But this is no surprise. This is our daily reality. We see it around us everyday and on the news: cloning, gene manipulation, e-mail, the Internet, Mars rovers, electric cars, hybrids, laser surgery, CD-ROMs, DVDs. All around us we see the wheels of progress turning: New discoveries, new technologies, a new societal knowledge and information base. New jobs are being created

Higher-Level Thinking Questions for Personal and Social Skills
Kagan Publishing • 1 (800) 933-2667 • www.KaganOnline.com

today in fields that simply didn't exist yesterday.

How do we best prepare our students for this uncertain future—a future in which the only constant will be change? As we are propelled into a world of ever-increasing change, what is the relative value of teaching students facts versus thinking skills? This point becomes even more salient when we realize that students cannot master everything, and many facts will soon become obsolete. Facts become outdated or irrelevant. Thinking skills are for a lifetime. Increasingly, how we define educational success will be away from the quantity of information mastered. Instead, we will define success as our students' ability to generate questions, apply, synthesize, predict, evaluate, compare, categorize.

If we as a professionals are to proactively respond to these societal shifts, thinking skills will become central to our curriculum. Whether we teach thinking skills directly, or we integrate them into our curriculum, the power to think is the greatest gift we can give our students!

We believe the questions you will find in this book are a step in the direction of preparing students for lifelong success. The goal is to develop independent thinkers who are critical and creative, regardless of the content. We hope the books in this series are more than sets of questions. We provide them as a model approach to questioning in the classroom.

On pages 8 and 9, you will find Questions to Engage Students' Thinking Skills. These pages contain numerous types of thinking and questions designed to engage each thinking skill. As you make your own questions for your students with your own content, use these question starters to help you frame

> # Virtually the only predictable trend is continuing change.
> — Dr. Linda Tsantis, Creating the Future

your questions to stimulate various facets of your students' thinking skills. Also let your students use these question starters to generate their own higher-level thinking questions about the curriculum.

Who?
Who is this book for?

This book is for you and your students, but mostly for your students. It is designed to help make your job easier. Inside you will find hundreds of ready-to-use reproducible questions. Sometimes in the press for time we opt for what is easy over what is best. These books attempt to make easy what is best. In this treasure chest, you will find hours and hours of timesaving ready-made questions and activities.

Place Higher-Level Thinking In Your Students' Hands

As previously mentioned, this book is even more for your students than for you. As teachers, we ask a tremendous number of questions. Primary teachers ask 3.5 to 6.5 questions per minute! Elementary teachers average 348 questions a day. How many questions would you predict our students ask? Researchers asked this question. What they found was shocking: Typical students ask approximately one question per month.* One question per month!

Although this study may not be representative of your classroom, it does suggest that in general, as teachers we are missing out on a very powerful force—student-generated questions. The capacity to answer higher-level thinking questions is

---

* Myra & David Sadker, "Questioning Skills" in *Classroom Teaching Skills*, 2nd ed. Lexington, MA: D.C. Heath & Co., 1982.

Higher-Level Thinking Questions for Personal and Social Skills
Kagan Publishing • 1 (800) 933-2667 • www.KaganOnline.com

7

Questions to Engage Students' Thinking Skills

Analyzing
- How could you break down…?
- What components…?
- What qualities/characteristics…?

Applying
- How is ____ an example of…?
- What practical applications…?
- What examples…?
- How could you use…?
- How does this apply to…?
- In your life, how would you apply…?

Assessing
- By what criteria would you assess…?
- What grade would you give…?
- How could you improve…?

Augmenting/Elaborating
- What ideas might you add to…?
- What more can you say about…?

Categorizing/Classifying/Organizing
- How might you classify…?
- If you were going to categorize…?

Comparing/Contrasting
- How would you compare…?
- What similarities…?
- What are the differences between…?
- How is ____ different…?

Connecting/Associating
- What do you already know about…?
- What connections can you make between…?
- What things do you think of when you think of…?

Decision-Making
- How would you decide…?
- If you had to choose between…?

Defining
- How would you define…?
- In your own words, what is…?

Describing/Summarizing
- How could you describe/summarize…?
- If you were a reporter, how would you describe…?

Determining Cause/Effect
- What is the cause of…?
- How does ____ effect ____?
- What impact might…?

Drawing Conclusions/ Inferring Consequences
- What conclusions can you draw from…?
- What would happen if…?
- What would have happened if…?
- If you changed ____, what might happen?

Eliminating
- What part of ____ might you eliminate?
- How could you get rid of…?

Evaluating
- What is your opinion about…?
- Do you prefer…?
- Would you rather…?
- What is your favorite…?
- Do you agree or disagree…?
- What are the positive and negative aspects of…?
- What are the advantages and disadvantages…?
- If you were a judge…?
- On a scale of 1 to 10, how would you rate…?
- What is the most important…?
- Is it better or worse…?

Explaining
- How can you explain…?
- What factors might explain…?

Higher-Level Thinking Questions for Personal and Social Skills
Kagan Publishing • 1 (800) 933-2667 • www.KaganOnline.com

Experimenting
• How could you test...?
• What experiment could you do to...?

Generalizing
• What general rule can...?
• What principle could you apply...?
• What can you say about all...?

Interpreting
• Why is _____ important?
• What is the significance of...?
• What role...?
• What is the moral of...?

Inventing
• What could you invent to...?
• What machine could...?

Investigating
• How could you find out more about...?
• If you wanted to know about...?

Making Analogies
• How is _____ like _____?
• What analogy can you invent for...?

Observing
• What observations did you make about...?
• What changes...?

Patterning
• What patterns can you find...?
• How would you describe the organization of...?

Planning
• What preparations would you...?

Predicting/Hypothesizing
• What would you predict...?
• What is your theory about...?
• If you were going to guess...?

Prioritizing
• What is more important...?
• How might you prioritize...?

Problem-Solving
• How would you approach the problem?
• What are some possible solutions to...?

Reducing/Simplifying
• In a word, how would you describe...?
• How can you simplify...?

Reflecting/Metacognition
• What would you think if...?
• How can you describe what you were thinking when...?

Relating
• How is _____ related to _____?
• What is the relationship between...?
• How does _____ depend on _____?

Reversing/Inversing
• What is the opposite of...?

Role-Taking/Empathizing
• If you were (someone/something else)...?
• How would you feel if...?

Sequencing
• How could you sequence...?
• What steps are involved in...?

Substituting
• What could have been used instead of...?
• What else could you use for...?
• What might you substitute for...?
• What is another way...?

Symbolizing
• How could you draw...?
• What symbol best represents...?

Synthesizing
• How could you combine...?
• What could you put together...?

Higher-Level Thinking Questions for Personal and Social Skills
Kagan Publishing • 1 (800) 933-2667 • www.KaganOnline.com

9

a wonderful skill we can give our students, as is the skill to solve problems. Arguably more important skills are the ability to find problems to solve and formulate questions to answer. If we look at the great thinkers of the world—the Einsteins, the Edisons, the Freuds—their thinking is marked by a yearning to solve tremendous questions and problems. It is this questioning process that distinguishes those who illuminate and create our world from those who merely accept it.

Make Learning an Interactive Process

Higher-level thinking is not just something that occurs between students' ears! Students benefit from an interactive process. This basic premise underlies the majority of activities you will find in this book.

As students discuss questions and listen to others, they are confronted with differing perspectives and are pushed to articulate their own thinking well beyond the level they could attain on their own. Students too have an enormous capacity to mediate each other's learning. When we heterogeneously group students to work together, we create an environment to move students through their zone of proximal development. We also provide opportunities for tutoring and leadership. Verbal interaction with peers in cooperative groups adds a dimension to questions not available with whole-class questions and answers.

> **Asking a good question requires students to think harder than giving a good answer.**
> — Robert Fisher, Teaching Children to Learn

Reflect on this analogy: If we wanted to teach our students to catch and throw, we could bring in one tennis ball and take turns throwing it to each student and having them throw it back to us. Alternatively, we could bring in twenty balls and have our students form small groups and have them toss the ball back and forth to each other. Picture the two classrooms: One with twenty balls being caught at any one moment, and the other with just one. In which class would students better and more quickly learn to catch and throw?

The same is true with thinking skills. When we make our students more active participants in the learning process, they are given dramatically more opportunities to produce their own thought and to strengthen their own thinking skills. Would you rather have one question being asked and answered at any one moment in your class, or twenty? Small groups mean more questioning and more thinking. Instead of rarely answering a teacher question or rarely generating their own question, asking and answering questions becomes a regular part of your students' day. It is through cooperative interaction that we truly turn our classroom into a higher-level think tank. The associated personal and social benefits are invaluable.

10

Higher-Level Thinking Questions for Personal and Social Skills
Kagan Publishing • 1 (800) 933-2667 • www.KaganOnline.com

When?
When do I use higher-level thinking questions?

Do I use these questions at the beginning of the lesson, during the lesson, or after? The answer, of course, is all of the above.

Use these questions or your own thinking questions at the beginning of the lesson to provide a motivational set for the lesson. Pique students' interest about the content with some provocative questions: "What would happen if we didn't have gravity?" "Why did Pilgrims get along with some Native Americans, but not others?" "What do you think this book will be about?" Make the content personally relevant by bringing in students' own knowledge, experiences, and feelings about the content: "What do you know about spiders?" "What things do you like about mystery stories?" "How would you feel if explorers invaded your land and killed your family?" "What do you wonder about electricity?"

Use the higher-level thinking questions throughout your lessons. Use the many questions and activities in this book not as a replacement of your curriculum, but as an additional avenue to explore the content and stretch students' thinking skills.

Use the questions after your lesson. Use the higher-level thinking questions, a journal writing activity, or the question starters as an extension activity to your lesson or unit.

Or just use the questions as stand-alone sponge activities for students or teams who have finished their work and need a challenging project to work on.

It doesn't matter when you use them, just use them frequently. As questioning becomes a habitual part of the classroom day, students' fear of asking silly questions is diminished. As the ancient Chinese proverb states, "Those who ask a silly question may seem a fool for five minutes, but those who do not ask remain a fool for life."

The important thing is to never stop questioning.
— Albert Einstein

As teachers, we should make a conscious effort to ensure that a portion of the many questions we ask on a daily basis are those that move our students beyond rote memorization. When we integrate higher-level thinking questions into our daily lessons, we transform our role from transmitters of knowledge to engineers of learning.

Where?
Where should I keep this book?

Keep it close by. Inside there are 16 sets of questions. Pull it out any time you teach these topics or need a quick, easy, fun activity or journal writing topic.

Higher-Level Thinking Questions for Personal and Social Skills
Kagan Publishing • 1 (800) 933-2667 • www.KaganOnline.com

11

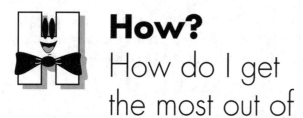

How?

How do I get the most out of this book?

In this book you will find 16 topics arranged alphabetically. For each topic there are reproducible pages for: 1) 16 Question Cards, 2) a Journal Writing activity page, 3) and a Question Starters activity page.

1. Question Cards

The Question Cards are truly the heart of this book. There are numerous ways the Question Cards can be used. After the other activity pages are introduced, you will find a description of a variety of engaging formats to use the Question Cards.

Specific and General Questions

Some of the questions provided in this book series are content-specific and others are content-free. For example, the literature questions in the Literature books are content-specific. Questions for the Great Kapok Tree deal specifically with that literature selection. Some language arts questions in the Language Arts book, on the other hand, are content-free. They are general questions that can be used over and over again with new content. For example, the Book Review questions can be used after reading any book. The Story Structure questions can be used after reading any story. You can tell by glancing at the title of the set and some of the questions whether the set is content-specific or content-free.

A Little Disclaimer

Not all of the "questions" on the Question Cards are actually questions. Some instruct students to do something. For example, "Compare and contrast…" We can also use these directives to develop the various facets of students' thinking skills.

The Power of Think Time

As you and your students use these questions, don't forget about the power of Think Time! There are two different think times. The first is the time between the question and the response. The second is the time between the response and feedback on the response. Think time has been shown to greatly enhance the quality of student thinking. If students are not pausing for either think time, or doing it too briefly, emphasize its importance. Five little seconds of silent think time after the question and five more seconds before feedback are proven, powerful ways to promote higher-level thinking in your class.

Use Your Question Cards for Years

For attractive Question Cards that will last for years, photocopy them on color card-stock paper and laminate them. To save time, have the Materials Monitor from each team pick up one card set, a pair of scissors for the team, and an envelope or rubber band. Each team cuts out their own set of Question Cards. When they are done with the activity, students can place the Question Cards in the envelope and write the name of the set on the envelope or wrap the cards with a rubber band for storage.

12

Higher-Level Thinking Questions for Personal and Social Skills
Kagan Publishing • 1 (800) 933-2667 • www.KaganOnline.com

2. Journal Question

The Journal Writing page contains one of the 16 questions as a journal writing prompt. You can substitute any question, or use one of your own. The power of journal writing cannot be overstated. The act of writing takes longer than speaking and thinking. It allows the brain time to make deep connections to the content. Writing requires the writer to present his or her response in a clear, concise language. Writing develops both strong thinking and communication skills.

A helpful activity before journal writing is to have students discuss the question in pairs or in small teams. Students discuss their ideas and what they plan to write. This little prewriting activity ignites ideas for those students who stare blankly at their Journal Writing page. The interpersonal interaction further helps students articulate what they are thinking about the topic and invites students to delve deeper into the topic.

Tell students before they write that they will share their journal entries with a partner or with their team. This motivates many students to improve their entry. Sharing written responses also promotes flexible thinking with open-ended questions, and allows students to hear their peers' responses, ideas and writing styles.

Have students keep a collection of their journal entries in a three-ring binder. This way you can collect them if you wish for assessment or have students go back to reflect on their own learning. If you are using questions across the curriculum, each subject can have its own journal or own section within the binder. Use the provided blackline on the following page for a cover for students' journals or have students design their own.

3. Question Starters

The Question Starters activity page is designed to put the questions in the hands of your students. Use these question starters to scaffold your students' ability to write their own thinking questions. This page includes eight question starters to direct students to generate questions across the levels and types of thinking. This Question Starters activity page can be used in a few different ways:

Individual Questions

Have students independently come up with their own questions. When done, they can trade their questions with a partner. On a separate sheet of paper students answer their partners' questions. After answering, partners can share how they answered each other's questions.

Higher-Level Thinking Questions for Personal and Social Skills
Kagan Publishing • 1 (800) 933-2667 • www.KaganOnline.com

13

JOURNAL

My Best Thinking

This Journal Belongs to

Higher-Level Thinking Questions for Personal and Social Skills
Kagan Publishing • 1 (800) 933-2667 • www.KaganOnline.com

Pair Questions

Students work in pairs to generate questions to send to another pair. Partners take turns writing each question and also take turns recording each answer. After answering, pairs pair up to share how they answered each other's questions.

Team Questions

Students work in teams to generate questions to send to another team. Teammates take turns writing each question and recording each answer. After answering, teams pair up to share how they answered each other's questions.

Teacher-Led Questions

For young students, lead the whole class in coming up with good higher-level thinking questions.

Teach Your Students About Thinking and Questions

An effective tool to improve students' thinking skills is to teach students about the types of thinking skills and types of questions. Teaching students about the types of thinking skills improves their metacognitive abilities. When students are aware of the types of thinking, they may more effectively plan, monitor, and evaluate their own thinking. When students understand the types of questions and the basics of question construction, they are more likely to create effective higher-level thinking questions. In doing so they develop their own thinking skills and the thinking of classmates as they work to answer each other's questions.

Table of Activities

The Question Cards can be used in a variety of game-like formats to forge students' thinking skills. They can be used for cooperative team and pair work, for whole-class questioning, for independent activities, or at learning centers. On the following pages you will find numerous excellent options to use your Question Cards. As you use the Question Cards in this book, try the different activities listed below to add novelty and variety to the higher-level thinking process.

Higher-Level Thinking Questions for Personal and Social Skills
Kagan Publishing • 1 (800) 933-2667 • www.KaganOnline.com

15

Activities

team activity #1

Question Commander

Preferably in teams of four, students shuffle their Question Cards and place them in a stack, questions facing down, so that all teammates can easily reach the Question Cards. Give each team a Question Commander set of instructions (blackline provided on following page) to lead them through each question.

Student One becomes the Question Commander for the first question. The Question Commander reads the question aloud to the team, then asks the teammates to think about the question and how they would answer it. After the think time, the Question Commander selects a teammate to answer the question. The Question Commander can spin a spinner or roll a die to select who will answer. After the teammate gives the answer, Question Commander again calls for think time, this time asking the team to think about the answer. After the think time, the Question Commander leads a team

discussion in which any teammember can contribute his or her thoughts or ideas to the question, or give praise or reactions to the answer.

When the discussion is over, Student Two becomes the Question Commander for the next question.

Question Commander

Higher-Level Thinking Questions for Personal and Social Skills
Kagan Publishing • 1 (800) 933-2667 • www.KaganOnline.com

Question Commander
Instruction Cards

Question Commander

1. Ask the Question: Question Commander reads the question to the team.

2. Think Time: "Think of your best answer."

3. Answer the Question: The Question Commander selects a teammate to answer the question.

4. Think Time: "Think about how you would answer differently or add to the answer."

5. Team Discussion: As a team, discuss other possible answers or reactions to the answer given.

Question Commander

1. Ask the Question: Question Commander reads the question to the team.

2. Think Time: "Think of your best answer."

3. Answer the Question: The Question Commander selects a teammate to answer the question.

4. Think Time: "Think about how you would answer differently or add to the answer."

5. Team Discussion: As a team, discuss other possible answers or reactions to the answer given.

Question Commander

1. Ask the Question: Question Commander reads the question to the team.

2. Think Time: "Think of your best answer."

3. Answer the Question: The Question Commander selects a teammate to answer the question.

4. Think Time: "Think about how you would answer differently or add to the answer."

5. Team Discussion: As a team, discuss other possible answers or reactions to the answer given.

Question Commander

1. Ask the Question: Question Commander reads the question to the team.

2. Think Time: "Think of your best answer."

3. Answer the Question: The Question Commander selects a teammate to answer the question.

4. Think Time: "Think about how you would answer differently or add to the answer."

5. Team Discussion: As a team, discuss other possible answers or reactions to the answer given.

Higher-Level Thinking Questions for Personal and Social Skills
Kagan Publishing • 1 (800) 933-2667 • www.KaganOnline.com

17

Fan-N-Pick

In a team of four, Student One fans out the question cards, and says, "Pick a card, any card!" Student Two picks a card and reads the question out loud to teammates. After five seconds of think time, Student Three gives his or her answer. After another five seconds of think time, Student Four paraphrases, praises, or adds to the answer given. Students rotate roles for each new round.

Spin-N-Think

Spin-N-Think spinners are available from Kagan Publishing to lead teams through the steps of higher-level thinking. Students spin the Spin-N-Think™ spinner to select a student at each stage of the questioning to: 1) ask the question, 2) answer the question, 3) paraphrase and praise the answer, 4) augment the answer, and 5) discuss the question or answer. The Spin-N-Think™ game makes higher-level thinking more fun, and holds students accountable because they are often called upon, but never know when their number will come up.

Three-Step Interview

After the question is read to the team, students pair up. The first step is an interview in which one student interviews the other about the question. In the second step, students remain with their partner but switch roles: The interviewer becomes the interviewee. In the third step, the pairs come back together and each student in turn presents to the team what their partner shared. Three-Step Interview is strong for individual accountability, active listening, and paraphrasing skills.

Team Discussion

Team Discussion is an easy and informal way of processing the questions: Students read a question and then throw it open for discussion. Team Discussion, however, does not ensure that there is individual accountability or equal participation.

Higher-Level Thinking Questions for Personal and Social Skills
Kagan Publishing • 1 (800) 933-2667 • www.KaganOnline.com

19

Think-Pair-Square

One student reads a question out loud to teammates. Partners on the same side of the table then pair up to discuss the question and their answers. Then, all four students come together for an open discussion about the question.

Question-Write-RoundRobin

Students take turns asking the team the question. After each question is asked, each student writes his or her ideas on a piece of paper. After students have finished writing, in turn they share their ideas. This format creates strong individual accountability because each student is expected to develop and share an answer for every question.

20

Higher-Level Thinking Questions for Personal and Social Skills
Kagan Publishing • 1 (800) 933-2667 • www.KaganOnline.com

Mix-Pair-Discuss

Each student gets a different Question Card. For 16 to 32 students, use two sets of questions. In this case, some students may have the same question which is OK. Students get out of their seats and mix around the classroom. They pair up with a partner. One partner reads his or her Question Card and the other answers. Then they switch roles. When done they trade cards and find a new partner. The process is repeated for a predetermined amount of time. The rule is students cannot pair up with the same partner twice. Students may get the same questions twice or more, but each time it is with a new partner. This strategy is a fun, energizing way to ask and answer questions.

Think-Pair-Share

Think-Pair-Share is teacher-directed. The teacher asks the question, then gives students think time. Students then pair up to share their thoughts about the question. After the pair discussion, one student is called on to share with the class what was shared in his or her pair. Think-Pair-Share does not provide as much active participation for students as Think-Pair-Square because only one student is called upon at a time, but is a nice way to do whole-class sharing.

Higher-Level Thinking Questions for Personal and Social Skills
Kagan Publishing • 1 (800) 933-2667 • www.KaganOnline.com

21

Inside-Outside Circle

Each student gets a Question Card. Half of the students form a circle facing out. The other half forms a circle around the inside circle; each student in the outside circle faces one student in the inside circle. Students in the outside circle ask inside circle students a question. After the inside circle students answer the question, students switch roles questioning and answering. After both have asked and answered a question, they each praise the other's answers and then hold up a hand indicating they are finished. When most students have a hand up, have students trade cards with their partner and rotate to a new partner. To rotate, tell the outside circle to move to the left. This format is a lively and enjoyable way to ask questions and have students listen to the thinking of many classmates.

Question & Answer

This might sound familiar: Instead of giving students the Question Cards, the teacher asks the questions and calls on one student at a time to answer. This traditional format eliminates simultaneous, cooperative interaction, but may be good for introducing younger students to higher-level questions.

Higher-Level Thinking Questions for Personal and Social Skills
Kagan Publishing • 1 (800) 933-2667 • www.KaganOnline.com

Numbered Heads Together

Students number off in their teams so that every student has a number. The teacher asks a question. Students put their "heads together" to discuss the question. The teacher then calls on a number and selects a student with that number to share what his or her team discussed.

RallyRobin

Each pair gets a set of Question Cards. Student A in the pair reads the question out loud to his or her partner. Student B answers. Partners take turns asking and answering each question.

Higher-Level Thinking Questions for Personal and Social Skills
Kagan Publishing • 1 (800) 933-2667 • www.KaganOnline.com

23

Pair Discussion

Partners take turns asking the question. The pair then discusses the answer together. Unlike RallyRobin, students discuss the answer. Both students contribute to answering and to discussing each other's ideas.

Question-Write-Share-Discuss

One partner reads the Question Card out loud to his or her teammate. Both students write down their ideas. Partners take turns sharing what they wrote. Partners discuss how their ideas are similar and different.

Higher-Level Thinking Questions for Personal and Social Skills
Kagan Publishing • 1 (800) 933-2667 • www.KaganOnline.com

Journal Writing

Students pick one Question Card and make a journal entry or use the question as the prompt for an essay or creative writing. Have students share their writing with a partner or in turn with teammates.

Independent Answers

Students each get their own set of Questions Cards. Pairs or teams can share a set of questions, or the questions can be written on the board or put on the overhead projector. Students work by themselves to answer the questions on a separate sheet of paper. When done, students can compare their answers with a partner, teammates, or the whole class.

Higher-Level Thinking Questions for Personal and Social Skills
Kagan Publishing • 1 (800) 933-2667 • www.KaganOnline.com

25

Center Ideas

1. Question Card Center

At one center, have the Question Cards and a Spin-N-Think™ spinner, Question Commander instruction card, or Fan-N-Pick instructions. Students lead themselves through the thinking questions. For individual accountability, have each student record their own answer for each question.

2. Journal Writing Center

At a second center, have a Journal Writing activity page for each student. Students can discuss the question with others at their center, then write their own journal entry. After everyone is done writing, students share what they wrote with other students at their center.

3. Question Starters Center

At a third center, have a Question Starters page. Split the students at the center into two groups. Have both groups create thinking questions using the Question Starters activity page. When the groups are done writing their questions, they trade questions with the other group at their center. When done answering each other's questions, two groups pair up to compare their answers.

Higher-Level Thinking Questions for Personal and Social Skills
Kagan Publishing • 1 (800) 933-2667 • www.KaganOnline.com

All About Me

higher-level thinking questions

Higher-Level Thinking Questions for Personal and Social Skills
Kagan Publishing • 1 (800) 933-2667 • www.KaganOnline.com

27

"Nine tenths of education is encouragement.

— Anatole France

Higher-Level Thinking Questions for Personal and Social Skills
Kagan Publishing • 1 (800) 933-2667 • www.KaganOnline.com

All About Me
Question Cards

All About Me

1 A friend of yours has never met your family. How would you describe your family or individual members?

All About Me

2 What is the best gift you ever received? Who gave it to you? When did you get it? Why was it so special?

All About Me

3 What is your all-time favorite memory? Why do you cherish it so?

All About Me

4 Who is the most important person or persons in your life? What do you do when you are together?

Higher-Level Thinking Questions for Personal and Social Skills
Kagan Publishing • 1 (800) 933-2667 • www.KaganOnline.com

29

All About Me
Question Cards

All About Me

5 What is the scariest thing you've ever been through? Why was it so scary for you?

All About Me

6 What is the most embarrassing thing that's ever happened to you?

All About Me

7 If you could change one thing about yourself, what would it be? Why?

All About Me

8 Do you have a nickname? If so, what is your nickname? How did you get it? If not, what would you like people to call you other than your name?

Higher-Level Thinking Questions for Personal and Social Skills
Kagan Publishing • 1 (800) 933-2667 • www.KaganOnline.com

All About Me
Question Cards

All About Me

9 If you won the lottery, what would you do with the money?

All About Me

10 Name one item you own that best represents you. Why does it represent you best?

All About Me

11 How would you describe yourself to someone who has never met you?

All About Me

12 Who is your hero? How are you like your hero? How are you unlike her or him?

Higher-Level Thinking Questions for Personal and Social Skills
Kagan Publishing • 1 (800) 933-2667 • www.KaganOnline.com

All About Me
Question Cards

All About Me

13 If you could be anyone else for a day, who would you be? Why?

All About Me

14 If you could speak to anyone in history, living or dead, who would you want to speak with? What would you ask him or her?

All About Me

15 What is the craziest thing you've ever done?

All About Me

16 Forrest Gump said, "Life is like a box of chocolates. You never know what you're going to get." Make up your own life simile: "Life is like…" Explain your simile.

Higher-Level Thinking Questions for Personal and Social Skills
Kagan Publishing • 1 (800) 933-2667 • www.KaganOnline.com

All About Me

Write your response to the question below.
Be ready to share your response.

**What is your all-time favorite memory?
Why do you cherish it so?**

_____

_____

_____

_____

_____

_____

_____

_____

_____

_____

_____

_____

_____

_____

_____

_____

_____

_____

_____

_____

Higher-Level Thinking Questions for Personal and Social Skills
Kagan Publishing • 1 (800) 933-2667 • www.KaganOnline.com

33

All About Me

Question Starters

Use the question starters below to create complete questions.
Send your questions to a partner or to another team to answer.

1. What would you do if

2. What was

3. How would you feel

4. If you had to choose

5. In your life

6. How would you describe

7. Where would

8. Who is

Higher-Level Thinking Questions for Personal and Social Skills
Kagan Publishing • 1 (800) 933-2667 • www.KaganOnline.com

All About School

higher-level thinking questions

Higher-Level Thinking Questions for Personal and Social Skills
Kagan Publishing • 1 (800) 933-2667 • www.KaganOnline.com

35

"The secret in education lies in respecting the student.

— Ralph Waldo Emerson

All About School
Question Cards

All About School

1 How would your life be different if you never went to school?

All About School

2 What is your favorite thing to do during recess or break? Why?

All About School

3 Who is the best teacher you ever had? What made him or her the best?

All About School

4 Would you prefer to go to school all year with frequent breaks or would you prefer one long summer break?

Higher-Level Thinking Questions for Personal and Social Skills
Kagan Publishing • 1 (800) 933-2667 • www.KaganOnline.com

37

All About School
Question Cards

5 All schools should have uniforms. Do you agree or disagree? Explain.

6 Finish the following statement: "School is..."

7 Do you think it is important to do well in school to succeed in life? Why or why not?

8 What is one thing your teacher could do to make this class better?

Higher-Level Thinking Questions for Personal and Social Skills
Kagan Publishing • 1 (800) 933-2667 • www.KaganOnline.com

All About School
Question Cards

All About School

9 What do you think will be the most helpful thing for you to learn in school?

All About School

10 Do you want to go to college? If so, which one would you like to go to? If not, why not?

All About School

11 A genie says he will grant you three wishes relating to school. What are your three wishes?

All About School

12 What is your least favorite subject? What could you do to make it better for you?

Higher-Level Thinking Questions for Personal and Social Skills
Kagan Publishing • 1 (800) 933-2667 • www.KaganOnline.com

39

All About School
Question Cards

All About School

13 How much homework do you think is fair for your teacher to assign every night?

All About School

14 If you could add a new subject or take a new class, what would it be? What would you do? What would you learn?

All About School

15 Do you want to be a teacher? Why or why not?

All About School

16 What is your favorite school activity? Describe it. Why is it your favorite?

Higher-Level Thinking Questions for Personal and Social Skills
Kagan Publishing • 1 (800) 933-2667 • www.KaganOnline.com

All About School

Write your response to the question below.
Be ready to share your response.

Do you think it is important to do well in school to succeed in life? Why or why not?

_____
_____
_____
_____
_____
_____
_____
_____
_____
_____
_____
_____
_____
_____
_____
_____
_____
_____
_____
_____

Higher-Level Thinking Questions for Personal and Social Skills
Kagan Publishing • 1 (800) 933-2667 • www.KaganOnline.com

41

All About School
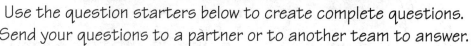
Question Starters

Use the question starters below to create complete questions.
Send your questions to a partner or to another team to answer.

1. If you were the principal

2. Why *do*

3. What problems

4. What would be different if

5. If you had a choice

6. What would you do if

7. How could you improve

8. What plans

Higher-Level Thinking Questions for Personal and Social Skills
Kagan Publishing • 1 (800) 933-2667 • www.KaganOnline.com

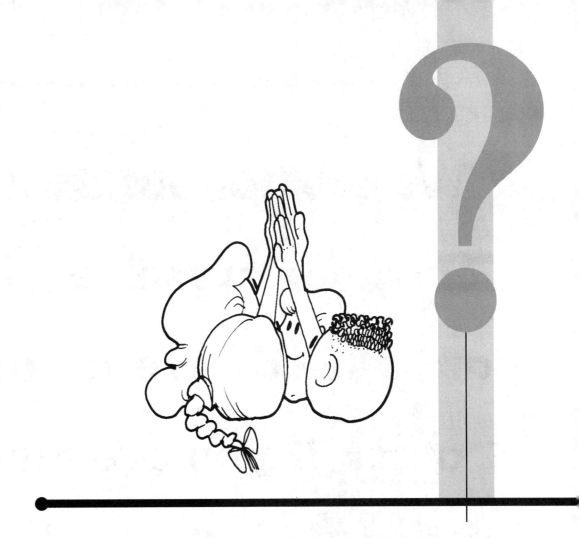

Caring and
Cooperation

higher-level thinking questions

Higher-Level Thinking Questions for Personal and Social Skills
Kagan Publishing • 1 (800) 933-2667 • www.KaganOnline.com

43

We are not put on this earth for ourselves, but are placed here for each other. If you are there always for others, then in time of need, someone will be there for you.

— Jeff Warner

Higher-Level Thinking Questions for Personal and Social Skills
Kagan Publishing • 1 (800) 933-2667 • www.KaganOnline.com

Caring and Cooperation
Question Cards

Caring and Cooperation

1 Two heads are smarter than one. Do you agree or disagree with this statement? Why or why not?

Caring and Cooperation

2 What is your dream job? In that job, how will you need to work with others?

Caring and Cooperation

3 Why do people care about each other? What would happen if no one cared about each other?

Caring and Cooperation

4 Do you consider yourself a good listener? How could you improve your listening skills?

Higher-Level Thinking Questions for Personal and Social Skills
Kagan Publishing • 1 (800) 933-2667 • www.KaganOnline.com

45

Caring and Cooperation
Question Cards

Caring and Cooperation

5 What is an act of kindness you did that you feel really good about?

Caring and Cooperation

6 Are the greatest accomplishments of the world done alone or with others? What general rule can you create?

Caring and Cooperation

7 What is the difference between friendship and love?

Caring and Cooperation

8 What does it mean to say, "The more love you give away, the more you have?"

Higher-Level Thinking Questions for Personal and Social Skills
Kagan Publishing • 1 (800) 933-2667 • www.KaganOnline.com

Caring and Cooperation
Question Cards

Caring and Cooperation

9 Put yourself in the place of someone else right now. Who are you? What are you doing? How do you feel? What are you thinking? What is it like to be that person?

Caring and Cooperation

10 Most of the major world religions have a golden rule such as: "Do unto others as you would have them do unto you." Why is this golden rule so important?

Caring and Cooperation

11 Who is your best friend? What makes you such close friends?

Caring and Cooperation

12 You are friendly to someone, but he or she is not friendly to you. Was it a mistake to be friendly?

Higher-Level Thinking Questions for Personal and Social Skills
Kagan Publishing • 1 (800) 933-2667 • www.KaganOnline.com

47

Caring and Cooperation

13 Could you ever like things about a person but not like the whole person? Explain.

Caring and Cooperation

14 What have you done with one or more other people that you are most proud of? What was it like working together?

Caring and Cooperation

15 When you cooperate with others, you often work toward the same goal. Name one time you cooperated with others. What goal did you share?

Caring and Cooperation

16 When working in a group, why is it sometimes helpful if people are very different?

Higher-Level Thinking Questions for Personal and Social Skills
Kagan Publishing • 1 (800) 933-2667 • www.KaganOnline.com

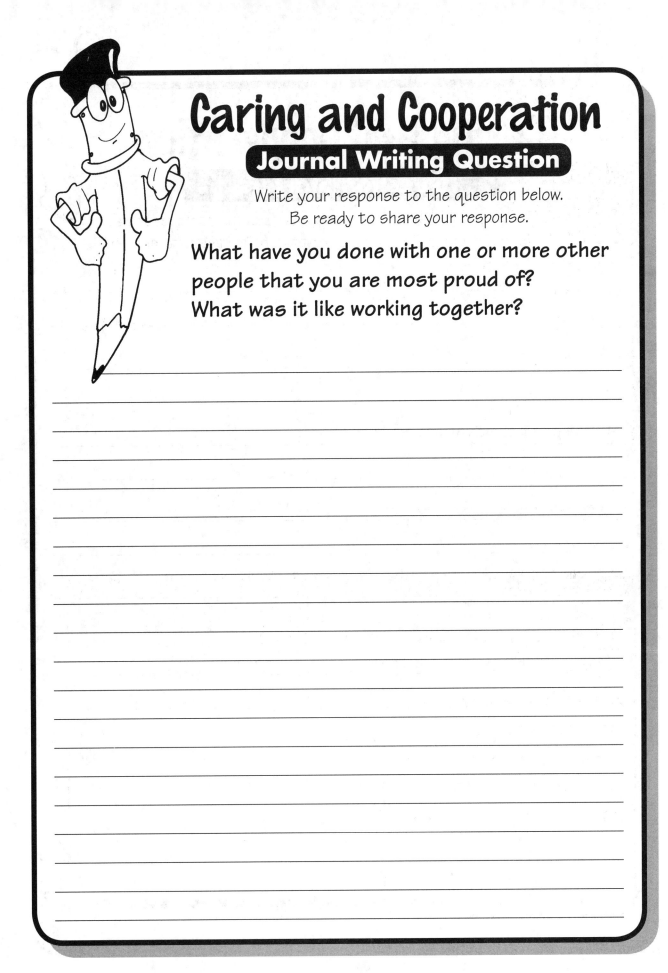

Caring and Cooperation

Journal Writing Question

Write your response to the question below.
Be ready to share your response.

What have you done with one or more other people that you are most proud of? What was it like working together?

Higher-Level Thinking Questions for Personal and Social Skills
Kagan Publishing • 1 (800) 933-2667 • www.KaganOnline.com

49

Caring and Cooperation
Question Starters

Use the question starters below to create complete questions.
Send your questions to a partner or to another team to answer.

1. Why is caring

2. Why is it important

3. What are the advantages

4. Who do you

5. If you had to

6. How is working with others

7. What would happen if

8. Would you rather

Higher-Level Thinking Questions for Personal and Social Skills
Kagan Publishing • 1 (800) 933-2667 • www.KaganOnline.com

Cheating

higher-level thinking questions

Higher-Level Thinking Questions for Personal and Social Skills
Kagan Publishing • 1 (800) 933-2667 • www.KaganOnline.com

51

"Do not do what you would undo if caught.

— Leah Arendt

Higher-Level Thinking Questions for Personal and Social Skills
Kagan Publishing • 1 (800) 933-2667 • www.KaganOnline.com

Cheating
Question Cards

Cheating

1 Have you ever cheated on a test? If so, how did it make you feel? If not, why not?

Cheating

2 You forgot to study for a vocabulary test. Your friend studied all night. You can see his test. Would you look at his answers? Why or why not?

Cheating

3 Is it ever okay to cheat? If so, when? If not, why not?

Cheating

4 What are some reasons someone would cheat?

Higher-Level Thinking Questions for Personal and Social Skills
Kagan Publishing • 1 (800) 933-2667 • www.KaganOnline.com

53

Cheating
Question Cards

Cheating

5 Is there a difference between cheating a little and cheating a lot, or is cheating cheating?

Cheating

6 If other people in your class were cheating on a test, would that make it more okay for you to cheat?

Cheating

7 Cheating is really cheating on yourself. Do you agree or disagree? Explain why.

Cheating

8 Do you know someone who cheats a lot? How do you feel about him or her?

Higher-Level Thinking Questions for Personal and Social Skills
Kagan Publishing • 1 (800) 933-2667 • www.KaganOnline.com

Cheating
Question Cards

Cheating

9 What would happen if everyone cheated and it was considered okay to cheat?

Cheating

10 What is the sneakiest way to cheat you've ever seen anyone use?

Cheating

11 If you could cheat and knew you'd never get caught, would you do it? Why or why not?

Cheating

12 Has anyone tried to cheat off you? Did you let him or her? How did it make you feel?

Higher-Level Thinking Questions for Personal and Social Skills
Kagan Publishing • 1 (800) 933-2667 • www.KaganOnline.com

55

Cheating
Question Cards

Cheating

13 If someone gets caught cheating, what do you think should happen to him or her?

Cheating

14 If you were the teacher, and you caught one of your students cheating on a test, what would you do?

Cheating

15 Have you ever been caught cheating? If so, what happened? If not, how would you feel if you got caught?

Cheating

16 What other ways do people cheat besides cheating on a test? Do you think people who cheat on tests are more likely to cheat in other ways?

Higher-Level Thinking Questions for Personal and Social Skills
Kagan Publishing • 1 (800) 933-2667 • www.KaganOnline.com

Cheating

Journal Writing Question

Write your response to the question below.
Be ready to share your response.

Cheating is really cheating on yourself. Do you agree or disagree? Explain why.

Higher-Level Thinking Questions for Personal and Social Skills
Kagan Publishing • 1 (800) 933-2667 • www.KaganOnline.com

57

Cheating

Question Starters

Use the question starters below to create complete questions.
Send your questions to a partner or to another team to answer.

1. Why is cheating

2. What would you do if

3. If you got caught

4. Would you

5. How would you describe

6. Have you

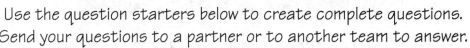
7. How would you feel if

8. What's more important

Higher-Level Thinking Questions for Personal and Social Skills
Kagan Publishing • 1 (800) 933-2667 • www.KaganOnline.com

Esteem
Builders

higher-level thinking questions

Higher-Level Thinking Questions for Personal and Social Skills
Kagan Publishing • 1 (800) 933-2667 • www.KaganOnline.com

59

"All the extraordinary men I have known were extraordinary in their own estimation.

— Woodrow T. Wilson

Higher-Level Thinking Questions for Personal and Social Skills
Kagan Publishing • 1 (800) 933-2667 • www.KaganOnline.com

Esteem Builders
Question Cards

Esteem Builders
1 What is one thing you have done or made that you are most proud of?

Esteem Builders
2 There is no one else in the world exactly like you. What makes you unique?

Esteem Builders
3 What is one thing you really enjoy doing?

Esteem Builders
4 Complete the following sentence. "I feel really good when…" Explain.

Higher-Level Thinking Questions for Personal and Social Skills
Kagan Publishing • 1 (800) 933-2667 • www.KaganOnline.com

61

Esteem Builders
Question Cards

Esteem Builders

5 Is there anything you do that you like to be by yourself? Explain.

Esteem Builders

6 What's more important to you: Your personal satisfaction or praise from others? Explain.

Esteem Builders

7 Have you ever won a contest, received an award or praise for your work? If so, what for? If not, what have you done that deserves recognition?

Esteem Builders

8 In your opinion, what are you good at doing?

Higher-Level Thinking Questions for Personal and Social Skills
Kagan Publishing • 1 (800) 933-2667 • www.KaganOnline.com

Esteem Builders
Question Cards

Esteem Builders

9 If you are feeling bad about yourself, what are some things you can do to boost your self-esteem?

Esteem Builders

10 Do you belong to any team, group, or club? Do you feel a sense of belonging? If not, what team or club would you like to belong to? Why?

Esteem Builders

11 Who is your best friend? What makes her or him your best friend?

Esteem Builders

12 What is one thing you would like to accomplish in your lifetime? Why is it a lifetime goal of yours?

Higher-Level Thinking Questions for Personal and Social Skills
Kagan Publishing • 1 (800) 933-2667 • www.KaganOnline.com

63

Esteem Builders

13 To feel good about themselves, some people change themselves to become who they want to be. Others accept themselves for who they are. Which do you identify with most?

Esteem Builders

14 What would the world be like if everyone looked and acted exactly the same?

Esteem Builders

15 Describe three positive qualities you have.

Esteem Builders

16 Sometimes people feel best about themselves when they do things for others. What is one nice thing you did for someone else?

Higher-Level Thinking Questions for Personal and Social Skills
Kagan Publishing • 1 (800) 933-2667 • www.KaganOnline.com

Esteem Builders

Journal Writing Question

Write your response to the question below.
Be ready to share your response.

There is no one else in the world exactly like you. What makes you unique?

_____

_____

_____

_____

_____

_____

_____

_____

_____

_____

_____

_____

_____

_____

_____

_____

_____

_____

_____

Higher-Level Thinking Questions for Personal and Social Skills
Kagan Publishing • 1 (800) 933-2667 • www.KaganOnline.com

65

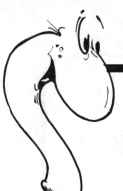

Esteem Builders

Use the question starters below to create complete questions.
Send your questions to a partner or to another team to answer.

1. How could you

2. Have you ever

3. How do you feel

4. What makes

5. Would you prefer

6. If you could

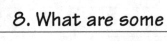
7. Who do you

8. What are some

Higher-Level Thinking Questions for Personal and Social Skills
Kagan Publishing • 1 (800) 933-2667 • www.KaganOnline.com

Feelings and Emotional Intelligence

higher-level thinking questions

Higher-Level Thinking Questions for Personal and Social Skills
Kagan Publishing • 1 (800) 933-2667 • www.KaganOnline.com

67

By starving emotions we become humorless, rigid and stereotyped; by repressing them we become literal, reformatory and holier-than-thou; encouraged, they perfume life; discouraged, they poison it.

— Joseph Collins

Higher-Level Thinking Questions for Personal and Social Skills
Kagan Publishing • 1 (800) 933-2667 • www.KaganOnline.com

Feelings and Emotional Intelligence
Question Cards

Feelings and Emotional Intelligence

1 How do you feel today? Why do you feel the way you do right now?

Feelings and Emotional Intelligence

2 Are you in touch with your emotions? Explain.

Feelings and Emotional Intelligence

3 What is one thing that really makes you happy? Why does it make you so happy?

Feelings and Emotional Intelligence

4 Have you ever completely lost control of yourself because your emotions were so strong? If so, what was the emotion and what happened?

Higher-Level Thinking Questions for Personal and Social Skills
Kagan Publishing • 1 (800) 933-2667 • www.KaganOnline.com

69

Feelings and Emotional Intelligence
Question Cards

Feelings and Emotional Intelligence

5 What are some things you can do to control your emotions when they get really strong?

Feelings and Emotional Intelligence

6 What was the most embarrassing moment of your life? Why was it so embarrassaing?

Feelings and Emotional Intelligence

7 When you try something and don't succeed, do you give up or try and try again? Give a specific example. What do you think about people who persist in the face of failure?

Feelings and Emotional Intelligence

8 When you feel unmotivated, what are some ways you can motivate yourself?

Higher-Level Thinking Questions for Personal and Social Skills
Kagan Publishing • 1 (800) 933-2667 • www.KaganOnline.com

Feelings and Emotional Intelligence
Question Cards

Feelings and Emotional Intelligence

9 Do you pay attention to the emotions of others? What are some benefits of tuning into other people's emotions?

Feelings and Emotional Intelligence

10 When were you really surprised? Why were you so surprised? What general statement can you make about the emotion "surprise"?

Feelings and Emotional Intelligence

11 Do you control your emotions, or do your emotions control you? Explain.

Feelings and Emotional Intelligence

12 Do you find it easy to make and keep friends? Why or why not?

Higher-Level Thinking Questions for Personal and Social Skills
Kagan Publishing • 1 (800) 933-2667 • www.KaganOnline.com

71

Feelings and Emotional Intelligence
Question Cards

Feelings and Emotional Intelligence

13 Have you ever been really, really sad? Describe what made you so sad and how you felt.

Feelings and Emotional Intelligence

14 When were you the angriest you've ever been? How did you handle your anger? Would you handle it differently if you had the chance?

Feelings and Emotional Intelligence

15 How can you become more aware of your feelings?

Feelings and Emotional Intelligence

16 Complete the following sentence. "Love is…"

Higher-Level Thinking Questions for Personal and Social Skills
Kagan Publishing • 1 (800) 933-2667 • www.KaganOnline.com

Feelings and Emotional Intelligence

Journal Writing Question

Write your response to the question below.
Be ready to share your response.

When were you the angriest you've ever been? How did you handle your anger? Would you handle it differently if you had the chance?

_____

_____

_____

_____

_____

_____

_____

_____

_____

_____

_____

_____

_____

_____

_____

_____

_____

_____

Higher-Level Thinking Questions for Personal and Social Skills
Kagan Publishing • 1 (800) 933-2667 • www.KaganOnline.com

73

Feelings and Emotional Intelligence

Question Starters

Use the question starters below to create complete questions.
Send your questions to a partner or to another team to answer.

1. When were you

2. If you were mad

3. Would you feel

4. Is happiness

5. What emotion

6. How would you feel if

7. How would you describe

8. Have you ever

Higher-Level Thinking Questions for Personal and Social Skills
Kagan Publishing • 1 (800) 933-2667 • www.KaganOnline.com

Lying and Honesty

higher-level thinking questions

Higher-Level Thinking Questions for Personal and Social Skills
Kagan Publishing • 1 (800) 933-2667 • www.KaganOnline.com

75

"No man, for any considerable period, can wear one face to himself, and another to the multitude, without finally getting bewildered as to which may be true."

— Nathaniel Hawthorne

Higher-Level Thinking Questions for Personal and Social Skills
Kagan Publishing • 1 (800) 933-2667 • www.KaganOnline.com

Lying and Honesty
Question Cards

Lying and Honesty

1 Have you ever told a lie? If so, do you regret lying? Why? If not, why not?

Lying and Honesty

2 Do you think it is ever okay to lie? Why or why not?

Lying and Honesty

3 Is it worse to lie to some people more than others, or is it equally bad to lie to anyone?

Lying and Honesty

4 If you would get in big trouble if you told the truth but knew a white lie could save you, what would you do?

Higher-Level Thinking Questions for Personal and Social Skills
Kagan Publishing • 1 (800) 933-2667 • www.KaganOnline.com

77

Lying and Honesty
Question Cards

Lying and Honesty

5 When I tell the truth, I feel big. when I lie, I feel small. Is this true for you too? Why or why not?

Lying and Honesty

6 If you make a habit of lying, people may not believe you anymore. Why is it important people believe you?

Lying and Honesty

7 Has anyone ever lied to you that you know about? If so, what about? How did it make you feel? In general, how do you think people feel about being lied to?

Lying and Honesty

8 Have you ever told a lie to avoid hurting someone's feelings? Is it a good thing to do?

Higher-Level Thinking Questions for Personal and Social Skills
Kagan Publishing • 1 (800) 933-2667 • www.KaganOnline.com

Lying and Honesty
Question Cards

Lying and Honesty

9 Honesty is the most important virtue. Do you agree or disagree? Explain.

Lying and Honesty

10 Lying is hard. You have to make up something to say, worry about being caught, and remember your lie. If honesty is so much easier, why do people lie?

Lying and Honesty

11 What would happen if everyone told lies all the time?

Lying and Honesty

12 Is there anyone who you know that would never lie to you? How do you feel about that person?

Higher-Level Thinking Questions for Personal and Social Skills
Kagan Publishing • 1 (800) 933-2667 • www.KaganOnline.com

79

Lying and Honesty

13 Is there a difference between little lies and big lies, or is a lie a lie? If you think there's a difference, describe it. If not, why not?

Lying and Honesty

14 If you were a parent and your son or daughter lied to you, how would it make you feel?

Lying and Honesty

15 Is not telling the whole truth the same as lying?

Lying and Honesty

16 If you exaggerate the truth, is that a lie? What's the difference between an exaggeration and a lie?

Higher-Level Thinking Questions for Personal and Social Skills
Kagan Publishing • 1 (800) 933-2667 • www.KaganOnline.com

Lying and Honesty
Journal Writing Question

Write your response to the question below.
Be ready to share your response.

If you exaggerate the truth, is that a lie? What's the difference between an exaggeration and a lie?

_____

_____

_____

_____

_____

_____

_____

_____

_____

_____

_____

_____

_____

_____

_____

_____

_____

_____

Higher-Level Thinking Questions for Personal and Social Skills
Kagan Publishing • 1 (800) 933-2667 • www.KaganOnline.com

81

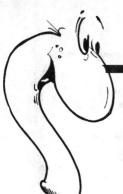

Lying and Honesty
Question Starters

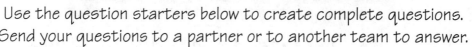

Use the question starters below to create complete questions.
Send your questions to a partner or to another team to answer.

1. Would you lie if

2. Is lying

3. Why is the truth

4. Have you ever

5. Why is it important

6. How would

7. Why do

8. How do you feel about

Higher-Level Thinking Questions for Personal and Social Skills
Kagan Publishing • 1 (800) 933-2667 • www.KaganOnline.com

Manners

higher-level thinking questions

Higher-Level Thinking Questions for Personal and Social Skills
Kagan Publishing • 1 (800) 933-2667 • www.KaganOnline.com

83

Manners are of more importance than laws. Manners are what vex or soothe, corrupt or purify, exalt or debase, barbarize or refine us, by a constant, steady, uniform, insensible operation, like that of the air we breathe in.

— Edmund Burke

Higher-Level Thinking Questions for Personal and Social Skills
Kagan Publishing • 1 (800) 933-2667 • www.KaganOnline.com

Manners
Question Cards

Manners

1 If an alien came down from outer space and wanted to learn good manners, what would you teach it?

Manners

2 Who is someone you know that has very good manners? How do you feel about that person?

Manners

3 Something that may be appropriate in one situation may not be appropriate in another situation. What are some examples?

Manners

4 What is the worst case of bad manners you've ever seen? What did you think of that person?

Higher-Level Thinking Questions for Personal and Social Skills
Kagan Publishing • 1 (800) 933-2667 • www.KaganOnline.com

85

Manners
Question Cards

Manners

5 Why do you think some people have very good manners and others have very bad manners?

Manners

6 On a scale of 1 to 100 (1 being terrible, 100 being terrific) how would you rate your own manners?

Manners

7 "Thank you" is a phrase that shows good manners. List four other polite words or phrases. Is it important for people to use these courtesies? Why or why not?

Manners

8 Why is it considered bad manners to spit or pick your nose in public?

Higher-Level Thinking Questions for Personal and Social Skills
Kagan Publishing • 1 (800) 933-2667 • www.KaganOnline.com

Manners
Question Cards

Manners

9 If bad words are just words, what is so bad about them? Do you use bad words often? Why or why not?

Manners

10 What would you consider bad table manners? What would you consider excellent table manners?

Manners

11 Do you ever talk badly about someone behind his or her back? How would you feel if someone was talking badly about you behind your back?

Manners

12 Do manners matter to you? Why or why not?

Higher-Level Thinking Questions for Personal and Social Skills
Kagan Publishing • 1 (800) 933-2667 • www.KaganOnline.com

87

Manners
Question Cards

Manners

13 If you see someone who is being rude, is it better to tell them they have been rude, or to just ignore them?

Manners

14 What would it be like if everyone had bad manners?

Manners

15 What would be a polite way to interrupt someone if they were in the middle of something?

Manners

16 How do you feel when someone is rude to you?

Higher-Level Thinking Questions for Personal and Social Skills
Kagan Publishing • 1 (800) 933-2667 • www.KaganOnline.com

Manners

Journal Writing Question

Write your response to the question below.
Be ready to share your response.

If an alien came down from outer space and wanted to learn good manners, what would you teach it?

Higher-Level Thinking Questions for Personal and Social Skills
Kagan Publishing • 1 (800) 933-2667 • www.KaganOnline.com

89

Manners
Question Starters

Use the question starters below to create complete questions.
Send your questions to a partner or to another team to answer.

1. How would you rate

2. What's worse

3. Why are manners

4. How would you describe

5. Who do you know

6. What is your opinion about

7. What should you

8. What would you consider

Higher-Level Thinking Questions for Personal and Social Skills
Kagan Publishing • 1 (800) 933-2667 • www.KaganOnline.com

Multiple Intelligences

higher-level thinking questions

Higher-Level Thinking Questions for Personal and Social Skills
Kagan Publishing • 1 (800) 933-2667 • www.KaganOnline.com

91

"Multiple intelligences generates a renewed respect for the uniqueness of each individual and the richness of our collective diversity.

— Spencer Kagan

Higher-Level Thinking Questions for Personal and Social Skills
Kagan Publishing • 1 (800) 933-2667 • www.KaganOnline.com

Multiple Intelligences
Question Cards

Multiple Intelligences
1 In what ways do you use your "art and picture smarts?"

Multiple Intelligences
2 What do you think is your strongest intelligence? Why?

Multiple Intelligences
3 What does it mean to be "self smart?"

Multiple Intelligences
4 What would the world be like if everyone was smart in the same way?

Higher-Level Thinking Questions for Personal and Social Skills
Kagan Publishing • 1 (800) 933-2667 • www.KaganOnline.com

93

Multiple Intelligences
Question Cards

Multiple Intelligences

5 What would be some advantages of being "nature smart?"

Multiple Intelligences

6 Do you think you are given a certain amount of smarts at birth or can you do things to make yourself smarter? What leads you to your conclusion?

Multiple Intelligences

7 What are the many ways a person can be smart?

Multiple Intelligences

8 In what ways do you use your "music smarts?"

Higher-Level Thinking Questions for Personal and Social Skills
Kagan Publishing • 1 (800) 933-2667 • www.KaganOnline.com

Multiple Intelligences
Question Cards

Multiple Intelligences

9 Do you consider yourself good at making and keeping friends? Why or why not?

Multiple Intelligences

10 What is your greatest skill using your "body smarts?" Describe.

Multiple Intelligences

11 If we are all smart in different ways, does it make any sense to say someone is smarter than someone else? Why or why not?

Multiple Intelligences

12 What is your favorite hobby? What smarts *do* you use when you *do* your hobby?

Higher-Level Thinking Questions for Personal and Social Skills
Kagan Publishing • 1 (800) 933-2667 • www.KaganOnline.com

95

Multiple Intelligences
Question Cards

Multiple Intelligences

13 Would you rather be kind of smart in lots of ways or super smart in just one way? Explain.

Multiple Intelligences

14 Which of your many smarts do you think needs the most work? What could you do to strengthen your weakest intelligence?

Multiple Intelligences

15 Who do you know who is smart in many ways? Explain how he or she uses his or her smarts.

Multiple Intelligences

16 Why is it important to be "word smart?"

Higher-Level Thinking Questions for Personal and Social Skills
Kagan Publishing • 1 (800) 933-2667 • www.KaganOnline.com

Multiple Intelligences
Journal Writing Question

Write your response to the question below.
Be ready to share your response.

What is your favorite hobby? What smarts do you use when you do your hobby?

Higher-Level Thinking Questions for Personal and Social Skills
Kagan Publishing • 1 (800) 933-2667 • www.KaganOnline.com

97

Multiple Intelligences
Question Starters

Use the question starters below to create complete questions.
Send your questions to a partner or to another team to answer.

1. How is being word smart

2. If you were really music smart

3. How could nature smarts

4. Is number smarts

5. Are art smart people

6. Is body smarts

7. Why do people smart people

8. How self smart

Higher-Level Thinking Questions for Personal and Social Skills
Kagan Publishing • 1 (800) 933-2667 • www.KaganOnline.com

My Favorites

higher-level thinking questions

Higher-Level Thinking Questions for Personal and Social Skills
Kagan Publishing • 1 (800) 933-2667 • www.KaganOnline.com

99

"Nothing is more difficult, and therefore more precious, than to be able to decide.

— Napoleon Bonaparte

My Favorites
Question Cards

My Favorites

1 What is your favorite song? What is the song about? What is the meaning of the song? Why do you like it?

My Favorites

2 Do you have a favorite TV show? What do you like about it? How would you categorize the show?

My Favorites

3 What is your favorite book? Describe the main character. Is she or he like or unlike you?

My Favorites

4 What is your favorite restaurant? What do you like to order when you eat there? Who do you usually go with?

Higher-Level Thinking Questions for Personal and Social Skills
Kagan Publishing • 1 (800) 933-2667 • www.KaganOnline.com

101

My Favorites
Question Cards

My Favorites

5 What is your favorite subject in school? What do you like about the subject? In what way will it prepare you for life?

My Favorites

6 What was your favorite vacation? What made it your favorite?

My Favorites

7 What is your favorite dessert? If you surveyed 100 people, how many would pick the same dessert?

My Favorites

8 What is your favorite kind of car? What does that tell us about you?

Higher-Level Thinking Questions for Personal and Social Skills
Kagan Publishing • 1 (800) 933-2667 • www.KaganOnline.com

My Favorites
Question Cards

My Favorites

9 What is your favorite sport? Do you prefer to play or to watch others play? How would you describe it to someone who's never played before?

My Favorites

10 Who is your favorite musical group? If you were going to write a magazine article about the band, what would you say?

My Favorites

11 What is your favorite animal? If you could switch places with that animal for a day, how would you spend the day?

My Favorites

12 What is your all-time favorite movie? If you were going to write the sequel, what would it be about?

Higher-Level Thinking Questions for Personal and Social Skills
Kagan Publishing • 1 (800) 933-2667 • www.KaganOnline.com

103

My Favorites
Question Cards

My Favorites

13 What is your favorite video game? If you were going to make a TV commercial for the game, what would the commercial be like? What channel would it be on? Who would be your target audience?

My Favorites

14 Who is your favorite actor? What would be some advantages of being her or him? What would be some disadvantages?

My Favorites

15 What is your favorite cartoon? What aspects of it make you like it better than other cartoons?

My Favorites

16 What is your favorite hobby? If you were going to write a how-to book, what chapters would your book have? What would be in the chapters?

Higher-Level Thinking Questions for Personal and Social Skills
Kagan Publishing • 1 (800) 933-2667 • www.KaganOnline.com

My Favorites

Journal Writing Question

Write your response to the question below.
Be ready to share your response.

What is your all-time favorite movie? If you were going to write the sequel, what would it be about?

Higher-Level Thinking Questions for Personal and Social Skills
Kagan Publishing • 1 (800) 933-2667 • www.KaganOnline.com

105

My Favorites

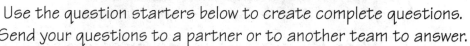
Question Starters

Use the question starters below to create complete questions.
Send your questions to a partner or to another team to answer.

1. What do your favorites

2. What is your favorite

3. What would you do if

4. Do your choices

5. If you could

6. What makes your favorite

7. What is your least favorite

8. If your favorite

Higher-Level Thinking Questions for Personal and Social Skills
Kagan Publishing • 1 (800) 933-2667 • www.KaganOnline.com

Positive Attitude

higher-level thinking questions

Higher-Level Thinking Questions for Personal and Social Skills
Kagan Publishing • 1 (800) 933-2667 • www.KaganOnline.com

107

Vote with your life; vote yes!

— Das Energi

Higher-Level Thinking Questions for Personal and Social Skills
Kagan Publishing • 1 (800) 933-2667 • www.KaganOnline.com

Positive Attitude
Question Cards

Positive Attitude

1 Optimists see the glass half full. Pessimists see the glass half empty. Are you an optimist or pessimist? Why?

Positive Attitude

2 Whether you think you can or think you can't, either way, you'll be right. What does this mean?

Positive Attitude

3 Who has the most positive attitude of anyone you know? How do you feel about her or him? How do other people feel about her or him?

Positive Attitude

4 Your attitude is your choice. Do you agree or disagree?

Higher-Level Thinking Questions for Personal and Social Skills
Kagan Publishing • 1 (800) 933-2667 • www.KaganOnline.com

109

Positive Attitude
Question Cards

5 How do the people you hang out with affect your attitude? In general, do your friends drag you down or bring you up? Explain.

6 Do you see the best in other people or do you look for the worst? Explain.

7 What does it mean to be a good sport? Do you consider yourself a good sport? Why or why not?

8 At times life can be difficult. But even when things don't seem so great, we have a lot to be thankful for. What are you thankful for?

Higher-Level Thinking Questions for Personal and Social Skills
Kagan Publishing • 1 (800) 933-2667 • www.KaganOnline.com

Positive Attitude
Question Cards

Positive Attitude

9 What are your life dreams? What would you like to do in your lifetime?

Positive Attitude

10 What would life be like if you always had a negative attitude?

Positive Attitude

11 Attitudes are contagious. Can you give an example?

Positive Attitude

12 Having a *good* sense of humor is helpful to maintain a positive attitude. How would you describe your sense of humor?

Higher-Level Thinking Questions for Personal and Social Skills
Kagan Publishing • 1 (800) 933-2667 • www.KaganOnline.com

111

Positive Attitude
Question Cards

Positive Attitude

13 List three adjectives of someone with a positive attitude. List three adjectives of someone with a negative attitude. Which list best describes you? Why?

Positive Attitude

14 If you had a friend who was really depressed, what could you do or say to cheer her or him up? Why would it cheer her or him up?

Positive Attitude

15 Do you forgive and forget or do you hold grudges or seek revenge?

Positive Attitude

16 Name three things that give you a bad attitude. What could you do so they don't drag you down?

Higher-Level Thinking Questions for Personal and Social Skills
Kagan Publishing • 1 (800) 933-2667 • www.KaganOnline.com

Positive Attitude
Journal Writing Question

Write your response to the question below.
Be ready to share your response.

At times life can be difficult. But even when things don't seem so great, we have a lot to be thankful for. What are you thankful for?

Higher-Level Thinking Questions for Personal and Social Skills
Kagan Publishing • 1 (800) 933-2667 • www.KaganOnline.com

113

Positive Attitude

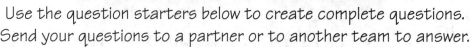
Question Starters

Use the question starters below to create complete questions.
Send your questions to a partner or to another team to answer.

1. Do positive people

2. How would you describe

3. What would you feel like

4. In your opinion

5. What really

6. What would it be like if

7. How would you rate

8. How could you improve

Higher-Level Thinking Questions for Personal and Social Skills
Kagan Publishing • 1 (800) 933-2667 • www.KaganOnline.com

Respect and Responsibility

higher-level thinking questions

Higher-Level Thinking Questions for Personal and Social Skills
Kagan Publishing • 1 (800) 933-2667 • www.KaganOnline.com

115

"Respect commands itself and it can neither be given nor withheld when it is due.

— Eldridge Cleaver

"We have a Bill of Rights. What we need is a Bill of Responsibilities.

— Bill Maher

Higher-Level Thinking Questions for Personal and Social Skills
Kagan Publishing • 1 (800) 933-2667 • www.KaganOnline.com

Respect and Responsibility
Question Cards

Respect and Responsibility

1 Do you think people have to earn your respect or do you automatically give people respect? Explain.

Respect and Responsibility

2 Everyone should respect their elders. Do you agree or disagree?

Respect and Responsibility

3 Many problems we see today are caused by a simple lack of respect. Why do you think it is so difficult for many people to respect others who are very different? How could we become more respectful of others?

Respect and Responsibility

4 Who do you respect more than anyone else? Why?

Higher-Level Thinking Questions for Personal and Social Skills
Kagan Publishing • 1 (800) 933-2667 • www.KaganOnline.com

117

Respect and Responsibility
Question Cards

Respect and Responsibility

5 What's more important to you: For others to respect you or for you to respect yourself?

Respect and Responsibility

6 If you were a parent and worked hard to raise your kids, would you expect them to respect you? What would you do if your kids didn't respect you?

Respect and Responsibility

7 Always respect authority. Do you agree or disagree with this statement? Explain.

Respect and Responsibility

8 What does it mean to be responsible? On a scale of 1 to 10 how would you rate how responsible you are? Explain.

Higher-Level Thinking Questions for Personal and Social Skills
Kagan Publishing • 1 (800) 933-2667 • www.KaganOnline.com

Respect and Responsibility
Question Cards

Respect and Responsibility

9 What responsibilities do you have in your family?

Respect and Responsibility

10 What responsibilities do you have in school?

Respect and Responsibility

11 What responsibilities do you have as a member of society?

Respect and Responsibility

12 Abraham Lincoln said, "You can't escape the responsibility of tomorrow by evading it today." What did he mean?

Higher-Level Thinking Questions for Personal and Social Skills
Kagan Publishing • 1 (800) 933-2667 • www.KaganOnline.com

119

Respect and Responsibility
Question Cards

Respect and Responsibility

13 Are you or have you ever been responsible for anyone else? If so, who and when? If not what would it be like to be responsible for someone else?

Respect and Responsibility

14 Have you ever decided to do something you wanted to do instead of something you were supposed to do? Explain. What happened?

Respect and Responsibility

15 What would happen if everyone decided to drop all their responsibilities?

Respect and Responsibility

16 Imagine you were a parent. What responsibilities would you have?

Higher-Level Thinking Questions for Personal and Social Skills
Kagan Publishing • 1 (800) 933-2667 • www.KaganOnline.com

Respect and Responsibility

Journal Writing Question

Write your response to the question below.
Be ready to share your response.

Many problems we see today are caused by a simple lack of respect. Why do you think it is so difficult for many people to respect others who are very different? How could we become more respectful of others?

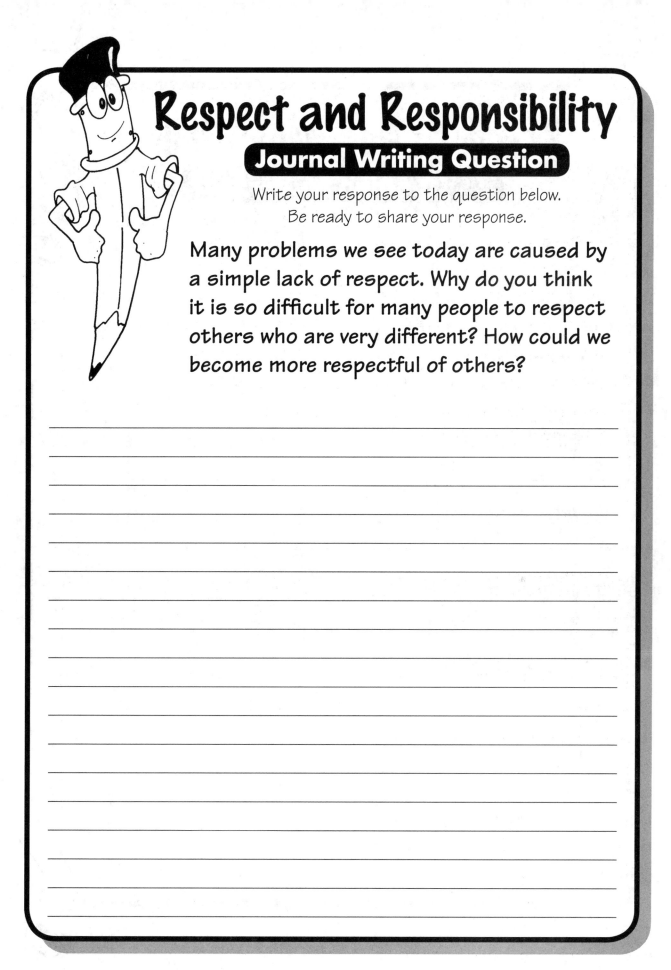

Higher-Level Thinking Questions for Personal and Social Skills
Kagan Publishing • 1 (800) 933-2667 • www.KaganOnline.com

121

Respect and Responsibility
Question Starters

Use the question starters below to create complete questions.
Send your questions to a partner or to another team to answer.

1. Would you respect _____

_____

2. How respectful _____

_____

3. If respect _____

_____

4. Would you lose respect _____

_____

5. If you were responsible _____

_____

6. What responsibilities _____

_____

 7. Why is it important _____

_____

8. How responsible _____

_____

Higher-Level Thinking Questions for Personal and Social Skills
Kagan Publishing • 1 (800) 933-2667 • www.KaganOnline.com

Safety

higher-level thinking questions

Higher-Level Thinking Questions for Personal and Social Skills
Kagan Publishing • 1 (800) 933-2667 • www.KaganOnline.com

123

"Intellectuals solve problems; geniuses prevent them.

— Albert Einstein

Higher-Level Thinking Questions for Personal and Social Skills
Kagan Publishing • 1 (800) 933-2667 • www.KaganOnline.com

Safety
Question Cards

Safety

1 Do you think kids under a certain age should be required to wear helmets when riding their bikes? What should the age be? How about when riding skates, skateboards, or in-line skates?

Safety

2 What would you do if there was an earthquake right now? Have you ever been in a big earthquake? What happened?

Safety

3 If you heard the school fire alarm go off, would you be scared? What would you do?

Safety

4 If you heard someone in your class brought a gun to school, what would you do?

Higher-Level Thinking Questions for Personal and Social Skills
Kagan Publishing • 1 (800) 933-2667 • www.KaganOnline.com

125

Safety
Question Cards

Safety

5 If you see your favorite cartoon character doing something crazy on TV, does that mean it's OK for you to do it too? How are you different from a cartoon character?

Safety

6 If a stranger pulled up next to you when you were walking home from school and asked you if you wanted a ride, what would you do?

Safety

7 What would you do if you found out your best friend was being abused by her father?

Safety

8 What would you do if you saw a strange vehicle next to your neighbors' house if they were away on vacation?

Higher-Level Thinking Questions for Personal and Social Skills
Kagan Publishing • 1 (800) 933-2667 • www.KaganOnline.com

Safety
Question Cards

Safety

9 What would you do if you were alone with an adult and all of the sudden he or she went into a seizure or had a heart attack?

Safety

10 Have you ever been in a situation where your safety was seriously threatened? If so, describe the situation. What did you do?

Safety

11 List three possible dangers in the kitchen. What can you do to reduce the risks in the kitchen?

Safety

12 What would you do if an older kid threatened to beat you up at recess if you didn't give him or her your lunch money?

Higher-Level Thinking Questions for Personal and Social Skills
Kagan Publishing • 1 (800) 933-2667 • www.KaganOnline.com

127

Safety
Question Cards

13 What would you do if you were playing in the park with some older kids and they offered you drugs?

14 If you were swimming at the beach and were being pulled out into the ocean by a riptide, what would you do?

15 What would you do if you heard a strange noise that sounded like whispers outside your bedroom window late at night?

16 What would you do if you were eating lunch with a friend and she or he started choking on a sandwich?

Higher-Level Thinking Questions for Personal and Social Skills
Kagan Publishing • 1 (800) 933-2667 • www.KaganOnline.com

Safety
Journal Writing Question

Write your response to the question below.
Be ready to share your response.

If you heard someone in your class brought a gun to school, what would you do?

_____

_____

_____

_____

_____

_____

_____

_____

_____

_____

_____

_____

_____

_____

_____

_____

_____

_____

Higher-Level Thinking Questions for Personal and Social Skills
Kagan Publishing • 1 (800) 933-2667 • www.KaganOnline.com

129

Safety

Question Starters

Use the question starters below to create complete questions.
Send your questions to a partner or to another team to answer.

1. How safe _____

_____

2. Why is safety _____

_____

3. What precautions _____

_____

4. What dangers _____

_____

5. What would you do if _____

_____

6. How could you prepare _____

_____

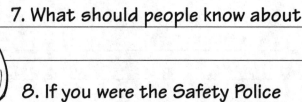

7. What should people know about _____

_____

8. If you were the Safety Police _____

_____

Higher-Level Thinking Questions for Personal and Social Skills
Kagan Publishing • 1 (800) 933-2667 • www.KaganOnline.com

Stealing

higher-level thinking questions

Higher-Level Thinking Questions for Personal and Social Skills
Kagan Publishing • 1 (800) 933-2667 • www.KaganOnline.com

131

"He who reigns within himself and rules passions, desires, and fears is more than a king

— John Milton

Stealing
Question Cards

1 Have you ever stolen anything? If so, what and where? How did you feel? If not, have you ever been tempted?

Stealing

2 What are some reasons people steal? Is it ever okay to steal?

Stealing

3 Robin Hood was known for stealing from the rich and giving to the poor. Do you respect him? Why or why not?

Stealing

4 What is the difference between stealing and borrowing? Is borrowing without asking the same as stealing?

Higher-Level Thinking Questions for Personal and Social Skills
Kagan Publishing • 1 (800) 933-2667 • www.KaganOnline.com

133

Stealing

5 Have you ever been caught stealing? If so, what happened? If not, how would you feel if you got caught?

Stealing

6 How would the world be different if no one ever stole?

Stealing

7 If you had a baby brother that asked you, "What does stealing mean?" What would you tell him?

Stealing

8 Stealing from a business is okay sometimes, but stealing from a person is never okay. Do you agree or disagree?

Higher-Level Thinking Questions for Personal and Social Skills
Kagan Publishing • 1 (800) 933-2667 • www.KaganOnline.com

Stealing
Question Cards

Stealing

9 Is sneaking into a movie the same as stealing from the movie theater?

Stealing

10 If someone steals from you, is it okay to steal from them?

Stealing

11 What do you think should happen to shoplifters that get caught?

Stealing

12 If you owned a business and you caught someone stealing from you, what would you do? How would you feel?

Higher-Level Thinking Questions for Personal and Social Skills
Kagan Publishing • 1 (800) 933-2667 • www.KaganOnline.com

135

Stealing
Question Cards

Stealing

13 Has anyone ever stolen something from you? If so, what? How did it make you feel? If not, what would you least want someone to steal from you?

Stealing

14 In some countries, if you get caught stealing, you get your hand chopped off. Is that fair? Why or why not?

Stealing

15 What would the world be like if stealing was acceptable and everyone did it?

Stealing

16 Is looking at someone's answers during a test the same as stealing? Why or why not?

Higher-Level Thinking Questions for Personal and Social Skills
Kagan Publishing • 1 (800) 933-2667 • www.KaganOnline.com

Stealing

Journal Writing Question

Write your response to the question below.
Be ready to share your response.

Has anyone ever stolen something from you? If so, what? How did it make you feel? If not, what would you least want someone to steal from you? Why?

Higher-Level Thinking Questions for Personal and Social Skills
Kagan Publishing • 1 (800) 933-2667 • www.KaganOnline.com

137

Stealing
Question Starters

Use the question starters below to create complete questions.
Send your questions to a partner or to another team to answer.

1. Is stealing

2. What would you do if

3. If you were a thief

4. Have you

5. If someone stole

6. How is stealing

7. Would you steal if

8. Why would

Higher-Level Thinking Questions for Personal and Social Skills
Kagan Publishing • 1 (800) 933-2667 • www.KaganOnline.com

Sticky Situations:

What Do You Do?

higher-level thinking questions

Higher-Level Thinking Questions for Personal and Social Skills
Kagan Publishing • 1 (800) 933-2667 • www.KaganOnline.com

139

"In any moment of decision the best thing you can do is the right thing, the next best thing is the wrong thing, and the worst thing you can do is nothing."

— Theodore Roosevelt

Higher-Level Thinking Questions for Personal and Social Skills
Kagan Publishing • 1 (800) 933-2667 • www.KaganOnline.com

Sticky Situations: What Do You Do?
Question Cards

Sticky Situations: What Do You Do?

1 All your friends come over to your house to spend the night. A friend suggests you get a bottle of your parents' liquor. What do you do?

Sticky Situations: What Do You Do?

2 You get two job offers for the summer. One pays a lot but is boring work. The other doesn't pay much but sounds exciting. What do you do?

Sticky Situations: What Do You Do?

3 You watching a movie in the theater. Two kids in front of you are being loud and obnoxious. You want to see the movie. What do you do?

Sticky Situations: What Do You Do?

4 You borrow your friend's bike without asking. You take it to the park and it gets stolen. What do you do?

Higher-Level Thinking Questions for Personal and Social Skills
Kagan Publishing • 1 (800) 933-2667 • www.KaganOnline.com

141

Sticky Situations: What Do You Do?
Question Cards

Sticky Situations: What Do You Do?

5 A bully at school picks on you every day. He says he'll beat you up if you tell on him. What do you do?

Sticky Situations: What Do You Do?

6 A boy or girl in your class asks you out for a date. You don't like him or her and don't want to go. What do you do?

Sticky Situations: What Do You Do?

7 You are having a sleep over. Everyone wants to toilet paper a neighbor's house. You don't want to. What do you do?

Sticky Situations: What Do You Do?

8 You are playing basketball at recess. You're not happy because your team is losing. The kid you are guarding shoots a basket. He looks at you and says, "In your face. You suck!" What do you do?

Higher-Level Thinking Questions for Personal and Social Skills
Kagan Publishing • 1 (800) 933-2667 • www.KaganOnline.com

Sticky Situations: What Do You Do?
Question Cards

Sticky Situations: What Do You Do?

9 You get an A on your math test. You notice that you missed three problems that your teacher didn't mark. The three wrong problems would give you a B. What do you do?

Sticky Situations: What Do You Do?

10 You are in a sunglasses store in the mall. You notice a man stealing a pair of sunglasses. What do you do?

Sticky Situations: What Do You Do?

11 You study hard for a test all night. In class, you see a classmate using a cheat sheet. What do you do?

Sticky Situations: What Do You Do?

12 You find a wallet in the park on your way home from school. It has $200 in cash and a driver's license. What do you do? Why?

Sticky Situations: What Do You Do?
Question Cards

Sticky Situations: What Do You Do?

13 You see some older kids picking on your younger brother's friend. You know if you stick up for him, you may get beat up. What do you do?

Sticky Situations: What Do You Do?

14 At school, a friend shows you graffiti he did. You get called into the principal's office because you were seen by the graffiti. What do you do?

Sticky Situations: What Do You Do?

15 Your parents tell you that you can bring your best friend with you to the circus. You have two best friends. What do you do?

Sticky Situations: What Do You Do?

16 You are failing social studies. You'll be grounded for a month if your parents find out. Your report card comes in the mail. You get it before your parents get home. What do you do?

Higher-Level Thinking Questions for Personal and Social Skills
Kagan Publishing • 1 (800) 933-2667 • www.KaganOnline.com

Sticky Situations: What Do You Do?

Journal Writing Question

Write your response to the question below.
Be ready to share your response.

A bully at school picks on you every day.
He says he'll beat you up if you tell on him.
What *do* you do?

_____

_____

_____

_____

_____

_____

_____

_____

_____

_____

_____

_____

_____

_____

_____

_____

_____

Higher-Level Thinking Questions for Personal and Social Skills
Kagan Publishing • 1 (800) 933-2667 • www.KaganOnline.com

145

Sticky Situations: What Do You Do?

Question Starters

Use the question starters below to create complete questions.
Send your questions to a partner or to another team to answer.

1. Peer Pressure: What would you do if

_____

2. Stealing: What would you do if

_____

3. Fairness: What would you do if

_____

4. Cheating: What would you do if

_____

5. Violence or Abuse: What would you do if

_____

6. Lying: What would you do if

_____

7. Drugs or Alcohol: What would you do if

_____

8. Any topic: What would you do if

_____

Higher-Level Thinking Questions for Personal and Social Skills
Kagan Publishing • 1 (800) 933-2667 • www.KaganOnline.com

Values

higher-level thinking questions

Higher-Level Thinking Questions for Personal and Social Skills
Kagan Publishing • 1 (800) 933-2667 • www.KaganOnline.com

147

"Try not to become a man of success but rather try to become a man of value."

— Albert Einstein

Values
Question Cards

Values

1 Who do you value most in your life? Explain why.

Values

2 Would you rather work hard all the time to succeed or kick back and relax?

Values

3 If you could be famous, would you want to be? If so, what would you want to be famous for? If not, why not?

Values

4 If your country asked you to fight in a war you did not believe in, would you?

Higher-Level Thinking Questions for Personal and Social Skills
Kagan Publishing • 1 (800) 933-2667 • www.KaganOnline.com

149

Values
Question Cards

Values

5 If you found out your friends were planning to spray paint the school on the weekend, would you turn them in? What would you do?

Values

6 Is there any cause you are willing to die for? Explain.

Values

7 Complete the following sentence: "Happiness is..."

Values

8 What thing that you own do you value most? What do you think it says about you as a person?

Higher-Level Thinking Questions for Personal and Social Skills
Kagan Publishing • 1 (800) 933-2667 • www.KaganOnline.com

Values
Question Cards

Values

9 Many people have values or beliefs that lead them through life. What values or beliefs do you have?

Values

10 People should be allowed to do anything they want in their own homes as long as it does not hurt anyone else. Do you agree or disagree?

Values

11 Your father looks troubled. You ask what's wrong. He says he can tell you something about himself but fears you will feel differently about him after he tells you. Do you want to know the truth?

Values

12 Rank order what you value:
1) world peace
2) being rich
3) being happy
4) being healthy
5) being loved
6) having integrity
Explain your ranking.

Higher-Level Thinking Questions for Personal and Social Skills
Kagan Publishing • 1 (800) 933-2667 • www.KaganOnline.com

151

Values

13 Would you rather make a lot of money selling drugs or be very poor working for a charity group?

Values

14 A spaceship lands in your backyard. You go outside and an extraterrestrial being offers to take you on a tour of the universe. The only problem is you can never return. Would you go?

Values

15 If you found out that your parents were in the Mafia, and wanted you to join, would you?

Values

16 If you had to choose between losing your best friend and losing a member of your family, who would you choose? Why?

Higher-Level Thinking Questions for Personal and Social Skills
Kagan Publishing • 1 (800) 933-2667 • www.KaganOnline.com

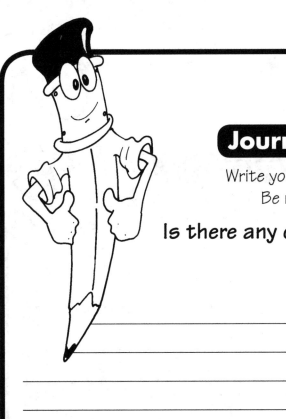

Values

Journal Writing Question

Write your response to the question below.
Be ready to share your response.

Is there any cause you are willing to die for?

_____

_____

_____

_____

_____

_____

_____

_____

_____

_____

_____

_____

_____

_____

_____

_____

_____

_____

_____

Higher-Level Thinking Questions for Personal and Social Skills
Kagan Publishing • 1 (800) 933-2667 • www.KaganOnline.com

153

Values

Use the question starters below to create complete questions.
Send your questions to a partner or to another team to answer.

1. What do you

2. If you had to

3. Would you rather

4. Should

5. What would you do if

6. Do you believe

7. If you had to choose

8. What values

Higher-Level Thinking Questions for Personal and Social Skills
Kagan Publishing • 1 (800) 933-2667 • www.KaganOnline.com

Notes

Kagan

It's All About Engagement!

Kagan is the world leader
in creating active engagement in the classroom. Learn how to engage your students and you will boost achievement, prevent discipline problems, and make learning more fun and meaningful. Come join Kagan for a workshop or call Kagan to **set up a workshop for your school or district**. Experience the power of a Kagan workshop. **Experience the engagement!**

SPECIALIZING IN:

★ **Cooperative Learning**

★ **Win-Win Discipline**

★ **Brain-Friendly Teaching**

★ **Multiple Intelligences**

★ **Thinking Skills**

★ **Kagan Coaching**

KAGAN PROFESSIONAL DEVELOPMENT

www.KaganOnline.com ★ 1(800) 266-7576